All Through Your Multiple Selves

Poems by Blake Edward Hamilton

LUCHADOR PRESS

Luchador Press
Big Tuna, TX

Copyright © Blake E. Hamilton, 2019
First Edition1 3 5 7 9 10 8 6 4 2
ISBN: 978-1-950380-71-8
LCCN: 2019954220

Design, edits and layout: El Dopa
Cover and title page images: Blake E. Hamilton
Author photo: Blake E. Hamilton
All rights reserved. No part of this publication may be reproduced or transmitted in any form or by any means, electronic or mechanical, including photocopying, recording or by info retrieval system, without prior written permission from the author.

Acknowledgments:

The poems in this collection are due in large part to one of those years that takes its place in the pantheon of the horrific. The support of many friends and family made an impactful difference. Thanks to my good friend and writing comrade, Sun Yung Shin, who invited me to the "Dark Side" early on in our friendship, and opened the gateway, so to speak. Anne Waldman, whose simple guidance to go in the direction of the unexpected, the anti-traditional, helped me uncover a pathway to much of the work here. Likewise, I am grateful to Sara Veglahn, a writing mentor and truth teller I was unbelievably lucky to have. My conversations with C.A. Conrad about movies, crystals, and tarot cards, amidst the larger conversation of writing, opened doors for me in terms of acknowledging authenticity in one's work. The same can be said about Eileen Myles, who taught me about the impact of emotional honesty during her readings and our very brief conversations. Rikki Ducornet, through our workshops and talks, helped me to understand how I arrive at my writing, and how to tap my own confidence, trusting the process. I am also extremely grateful to the larger community of writers and artists at Naropa University, and in Boulder, CO, where many of these poems found their way into existence.

-BEH

TABLE OF CONTENTS

Untitled / 1
Ghosts Hang Around Longer / 2
Home / 3
You Outstayed Your Welcome / 4
People Are Mostly Good / 5
Butterweed / 8
Morning People / 9
Only The Animal Is Natural / 11
Husband / 12
Blind Cavern / 15
21st Century Blues / 16
Famine / 17
Knife / 18
Loophole / 19
Neighborhood / 20
Field House, Abandoned / 22
The Turtle Pond / 24
Why Does Silence Feel Like A Wound? / 26
All Moods Are A Night Scare / 27
Gravitas / 28
Trophies For Effort / 29
What "Gay" Is / 30
Another Cock / 31
This Winter Isn't So Bad / 34
The Fire Exit Is My View / 35
You're My Past Life / 37

Untitled / 38

Untitled / 39

Arachnida / 40

Stem / 41

Wolf Boy / 42

Untitled / 44

Time Traveler / 45

The Reading Room Is Silent / 46

Home: Number 2 / 47

The Fleas / 48

Horses In the Mountains / 50

Your Worthlessness Costs The Most / 51

Bukowski / 52

The Vanishing / 54

Guillotine Ebullience / 55

Low Train Siren / 56

Like a painter who bends the treetops in order to capture a gust of wind on his canvas, sending hair and skirts flying, I could only ever manage to recall him by transporting me to myself, to the version from that time.

— Clarice Lispector, *Obsession*

The wounded man stared at the gap in the trees where they had disappeared. His rage was complete, consuming him as fire envelops the needles of a pine. He wanted nothing in the world except to place his hands around their necks and choke the life from them.

— Michael Punke, *The Revenant*

You were once made

to protect   to withstand

   functionality carved
   you lips, your tongue

   something to insert
   to press up into
   to connect, to function larger

   snug clip slot to accept
   vulnerable ends soaked

   a spout for your plastic
   mouth

GHOSTS HANG AROUND LONGER

There:

        Two
of me

        Three
of me

each spinning back on time, flattened,
crushing versions superior —

Can you give me a little help, please?

I'm not yet prepared for the maw.
Split me open, and you'll find the haunt.

Old forms dissolve the easiest,
self-contained, place as memory;

it's an integral narrative — so, see me age,

Ephemeral Footnote.

HOME

I prefer the desert;
it does not pretend

dry sun spines –
the architecture of bones

wreathed selenite, pelvic
chairs supporting orange

bluff debris, rattlesnake
mouths licking dust,

a permanent exhalation
crescent moon teeth

seeking a hide, the muscular
heft of a meaty hip

YOU OUTSTAYED YOUR WELCOME

Night with the obese
guy, all swill

boot loving, engorged
on toes

checking text messages
between my legs

and then the time
because we were running

out of it; your face
doesn't want to be seen

it finds ways
to deflect cream-

colored lips, bunched
brown,

cigarette paper soaked
on a stub

PEOPLE ARE MOSTLY GOOD

Poems about lovers
are attempts at honesty.

I want to tell this
to the man

at the laundromat
pressing, lovingly,

all of the coin return
buttons under the dryers,

a cloudy sandwich baggy
in his indignant fingers;

he sees me, clutches me
between the pinball machine,

the bouncy ball vendor,
a look meant

for the eviscerated,
for the politician,

and I wonder

if he's going to strangle
me with his bag

of stolen quarters,
but he leaves

and the man with the backpack
drinking a Sprite

barfs a river
over the spinning porthole

churning white with colorfast bleach;
he belches a high note,

then waddles back to stand
under the flat-screen

showing a crumpled mass
at the 40 yard line,

a woman behind the counter
writes down the plate

number of a customer
who will not move

out of the parking space
where others are trying to park;

he shouts to them that he's
not a retard!

and that they can ask him nicely,
only then will he move;

he squeezes cranberry
scented drier sheets

the color of pale valentines,
and taps into his phone.

BUTTERWEED

Breeches
Black rot

the dictionary,
red-backed

open in your
hands

from you
on a bad

day

        neither
of

        us

says

        hello

MORNING PEOPLE

The soulless include
early risers

jovial, discussing
learning strategies;

quiet village houses,
snow dusted peaks

shot in unapologetic
sun   shine,

lazy factory smoke
unspooling near

the edges of parking
garages –

somewhere through
windows of the dead,

wet crackling teeth
smile against a Cinna-

bon pastry, icing crammed
in tight, snappy grins,

oh what a joy
to greet a world in ice

with wide chews,
jaws jolting on a croissant,

and heavy sighs over
'fresh delicious creamy'

coffee, the exhale pop
of a virginal strawberry

between nicotine
molars

suck sucks sucking
it down, and all smiles

in front
of the gleaming

dry-rase board

ONLY THE ANIMAL IS NATURAL

The horse
is more powerful

than us
but we ride

it blind;
bone machines,

pulsing coat
and limbs raking

wide hoofs
into old

mouths, metal
gagged, lashing

muscle against
brutal light

HUSBAND

I end
up at psychic

gift shops
at the same time

on the same day
searching for candles,

feathers, and rocks,
carved crystals,

handbooks for love
and protection.

The soothsayer
takes Visa

when I tell
her about you,

and she offers
quiet spells;

some I take
and enact

at home
in the bath;

the plastic duck
lies on its back,

staring up at me
near my feet

through the bubbles;
the magic has faded:

you're no brighter
on Monday

than any other Monday,
your hands

have an invisible
pocket between

your khakied legs
while we talk

about buying houses,
ephemeral equity,

romance in the split;
we're playing house

too much. Our future
is everything you want;

its method of arrival
is indirect invitation

I'm drowning in black tourmaline
and lapis lazuli,

tumbled rose quartz,
searching for a hand,

which you manipulate
to dismantle maps

of your childhood –
your absence

is expensive
but I found you:

how often
are you found?

BLIND CAVERN

On the periphery
of odd selves,

of nature,
is a version

that seeks rough
consummation;

in liquid dark,
ocean-pitch,

symmetry of teeth — evolved for lightless pathways —

finds my eager,
naked leg

and tugs, swallowing,
a quiet request;

the start
of most obsessions

21st CENTURY BLUES

remove the name of a thing
and it begins to exist

excavations are stillborn,
unassuming histories

mined avenues stippled
in weary street lamps,

after the greatest cache
of salvaged mystery

only the weakest form
of dark, now; the runoff

of shadows. Doorways
hide sharp figures

everything is exposed
everything has a name

FAMINE

A thing that smiles
and bites off pieces
of you, smiling

lips upturned,
secret machinery;

the idea of a face
evolved over time

to appear kind.

All starving things
are kind.

KNIFE

Toughened;
bone roads

feet-steady
pale-white

smooth,
to the horizon.

Sun
and then dogs

hunt starved
mouths and tongues

dig mindless,
upend old

bullets and beaming
fingers

topsoil cut,
disposal marked

bodies cry
cracks bloom

LOOPHOLE

rotgut
cacti-fingers
spindled
brainwave
creak-shudder
rolling, toe-down
a body-spine,
lucrative wager,
a whisper
shoulder disruption
right at the center
of locution.

There's traffic
beyond the trees.

NEIGHBORHOOD

1.
Porch light
rendezvous

tree-whisper
suffocates the hush

bursting languid
over cicadas

panting rigorous
in cool yards

house-faces-house
glowing warm,

the color of pumpkin guts
edges under

low gray
clouds, air slips,

and shadows:
soft intrusions

2.
threesome at
4:00 am

cock all the way
down, electric

tongue, asses
round, pop

hairy center
gripping stomach

shouts final
jitter

impossible opening
I'm all over

the sheets
before the others,

laughing smell
in my face,

hard and leaving
the dark fumblings:

spurts I missed
when the sun came up

FIELD HOUSE, ABANDONED

My chest
wounds

are					finicky

Fingers snap
against

old					bone

All of my
Houses

are					haunted

They come
complete

with					ghosts

I have
Inhabited

every   desert

I have
Been

dead   on

old
roads

THE TURTLE POND

The small pond
At night

Has a body
In it –

It's me,
I'm at the bottom,

A meat-curiosity
For the turtles –

Lips of wind
Push tiny waves

Over their heads,
Black darts

Under the moon,
Cold-silver, insistent,

In the muck;
Only parts of me

Are illuminated,
A scaly finger, a brash toe.

The turtles
Are choosey,

Not impolite,
They're patient

Before they wrench
Off

An ear,
Or a testicle.

Their homes
Are on their backs,

Carried into
The darker parts,

Lightless holes,
Invaded only by them.

WHY DOES SILENCE FEEL LIKE A WOUND?

Like a rebuff, a knife at an angle.

My mouth is full of your sleep.

In the roots of my teeth are my indecisions.

I try to pacify the quake in my feet

By focusing on nature:

Its violence somehow asks less;

A tsunami is a gentle hand, a quick gesture

On its way to a dive,

Homes split like a hand on glass.

Rooms stay muffled, complete

Despite your rattling transgressions.

ALL MOODS ARE A NIGHT SCARE

a cyclical bone,

a rotten note in the sound waves –

it's at night my lungs

feel like raw glass, my teeth bloody,

the burn outside comes

from the streetlamps; they're always protecting

something, a patch of wet

cement, an abandoned basketball, like an orange

eye slanted in the gray;

all people are weak at night, slumming in the pits

of their own kitchens,

resting at the window to watch rain collect

GRAVITAS

Lung weight,
chest and back:

whip heavy, scarred
to clear maps,

carried like bricks
in a cold current,

a stream witnessed
by playing children;

front yard concrete,
tenement-building-nostalgia

here is more weight

the weight of displacement
our memories unknown

to gravity, but drifting;
our memories not our

own
the one above,

not mine

TROPHIES FOR EFFORT

So close
to the half-sprouted

suggestion
of an appendage,

like a thumb
that did not make it,

a rough protrusion,
hint of a nail, an arc

stopped mid-bow
graceful, unseen,

swallowed by breadth,
the rest of the hand

charging forward,
a body-ocean

burning off
old ambitions

WHAT "GAY" IS

has been told

to me. A stagnant
thing, like a crustacean

cemented, a marriage
of two stones at home

in black-deep – a schooner
built from a sea bed,

masked in starfish
limb over limb (cha cha cha),

mouth and anus flexing,
flashing the other fish;

in this opening, nature
was showing off

an aptitude for expediency.

ANOTHER COCK

        Another cock
in my mouth
        in my bed
in my hand
        another
in my bed
        in my mouth
stupid eager
        in my bed
spurt drive
        in my hand
sack drop
        eager
generated
            spurt   drive
spume dust
        gen   er   ated
sheet quagmire
    dust
devastation soap

in lonely showers
        sheet quagmire
washing cock
        lonely
off of my cock

off of my thighs
    shower devastation

off of my
                soap

                sack

off of my

                off

                        my

spurt drive

gen
dust

sheet
lonely

devastation

THIS WINTER ISN'T SO BAD

more like phlegm
or a cataract

draped over old
buildings and derelict

parks with picnic
benches vacant

of bodies, sitting
open like palms

in grass waiting,
receiving gray

mist, a fish mouth hanging
open, expectant

even if nothing comes,
just wind brushing

the corners of panic
rooms,

the moon in the haze.

THE FIRE EXIT IS MY VIEW

Its red, swollen
warning faces me

from another door
and invites me

to push through so I can
get out of here,

only it won't
be my fault

this time:
There are fires.

Hell. Big, present;
bombastic shower

of blister-skin over
both ends of me --

torched, flame-fondled;
some burns are familiar,

some stay around
so you'll recognize them

at certain functions,
like this one:

The space between
me and the escape

is an event meant
as a kindness,

a caveat,
a note to self.

YOU'RE MY PAST-LIFE;

we gifted microbes then, too.

Look at us, we don't
know what parts

of ourselves we need
to open, to insert –

Our new incarnation
has left us with gaps

too vast and permanent,
immune to the standard

ropes and bridges that carry
tribes, families, and rough

dogs leaping at loose cords;
we had our fantasy

we should be grateful,
we had a whole life together.

Neither of us recognizes it.

I have found ways through new languages, old pathways, neural corridors, leading snake-like from the center of time, a patch of earth traumatized into replay, a reverberation from skull-base to crown; a voice calls from the dark, your voice, like a signal, a hint on a map – I've known you before, my biggest horror come to life – here is the rickety bed, the cheap desk, lights draped over the walls, salt-lamp glow, only in this form we're prevented from destroying each other; saved by a gulf, an unintended reprimand for briefly loving, your hand dividing parts of me, when you go. It's a new start – I can be shed, you can slither out of me, residual crinkle of scales, energetic shimmer, I can toss and turn, thrown to the sands, accoutrements for the sagebrush, a tentative home for something smaller looking for a respite, camouflage from the enemies located in safe places, always the least expected, ready to jump at the gentlest movement.

I'm reborn in my own sickness, the world is slow and too bright. I am a reduced, glowing thing. I feel pink and raw. The pressure in my ears, my eyes, goes through me like a barbell.

A bastion of illness. There aren't enough blow-jobs to heal this.

A bitch in a red coat and shorts coughing directly into the room.

I jam sharp things into my gums.

Lips and a jawline.

Armpit dick.

It has to be this way.

ARACHNIDA

Web-filament
corner window
cold sun

bouncing light
point-to-point
where an intention

might have been;
the start of a home,
an innocuous, 90-degree angle,

remnant shape —
nothing special,
free of bodies,

caught in its center
no guests to stay
and comment on the warmth

the square-footage
the hidden rooms

STEM

A broken back

starts with generosity

starts with a hug

a hand slipped

    around the cusp

    around the cranium

orbiting distant shatters

realms stunted in kindness

crossing cold distance to head-lock

crossing body-width to fevers

stand peeled, rind jowls, weak eyes

stand knock-kneed, redolent disaster

WOLF BOY

    My call
            is more
  animal
       groan

       a whimper
  from a box,
       a frozen plug

  I can't sustain
        seduction
  I can't lure
       Wolves with my bait

scent glands
      excrete weak
party favors
      pussy cakes, mashed

I hunt corporate
      food chains
I gobble corporate

        portioning
Men who lie
    to themselves
eat the blind
    the most

My dreams are portents lately; everyone in them brings a warning but I don't ever get to the warning – one, a blond woman, keeps giving me pottery – the look on her face is stern, like a lake at five AM, no movement, no surface giveaways, just stillness; I have so many bowls from her, stockpiled somewhere between here and a REM state. I wonder if they'll come in handy later, or give a clue to my dread, which hovers like a deer corpse, upright, staring blank, right at me through the trees, through cold Aspens – in the other dream, I'm invited somewhere and another woman pleads with me to take something; I don't get to know, either, just the dread, just the blank stare.

TIME TRAVELER

I keep going back

to repeat steps

to see if I can

do it all over again

with no trip-ups

no more blind trust

just paths like burns

places I existed

reflected back at me

while I'm just

biding my time

THE READING ROOM IS SILENT

the passageway before the doors
is clear

chairs arranged, unattended

through the glass, wide views
of burned tress

singed cold

places of hard memory, welded
into the grass

we have been here before

is that enough?
To have been someplace?

HOME: NUMBER 2

I'm always in the wrong
forest; that's how it begins,
maniacal seeking, rabid jaunt,
refugee sprinting to the next
home

Cave walls, this one; eroded.
By everyone else's standards:
A ghost body, ectoplasmic
Christmas carols, vocal chords
strained, cat's claws

THE FLEAS

The fleas
want to sleep
with me.

Black snag bodies
soften

the thread count,
catapulting | weightless

into hairy sweets,
skin-fold effluvium,

a dance in warm cavern thatches,
and needy stink gaps.

|\ | /   \|

My generously stippled
ankles are pale bone slopes

for machine mouths
to meet and to suck.

They're quiet
about things, at least.

Many families are quiet
about hunger, and its acts;

tiny invasions
best achieved in the dark,

under beds with
hands over mouths.

HORSES IN THE MOUNTAINS

clouds rushing through a smokestack,
early morning fog bank, trees, daggers;
the steady tap of rain,

the measured thump
of the quiet

the house
with wooden floors

YOUR WORTHLESSNESS COSTS THE MOST.

Real death moving
hollow to the core;

here is the sun,
the desert,

here, among the cacti,
is us

our remains
our sounds brushed silent

hushed into
the expanse,

the place
where we stop

BUKOWSKI

Un-Sainted at the Detritus Carnival.

I want to tell you,
people are still trash;

they just worship
themselves more,

and snap photos
of their food,

their sagging labia,
and their small dicks.

Everyone is a god today;
it's exhausting.

Snap snap, snap snap.

The woman at the table
next to me

wears a shirt
of rotting fruit designs.

Ma'am! Ma'am! she shouts.

I want to tab-out! OKAY?!

She snarls. To the bald man
across from her.

Snap snap.

Her ankles are stippled
in razor burn.

All dogs on sidewalks
starve these days; I just wanted

to tell you.

THE VANISHING

There is a man
in a red shirt

wandering among sand
dunes, arms sawing;

he walks to the trees,
then deeper, then

becomes tiny, and
disappears.

The course is empty
again; trees battle

phone lines, stretching
over the 9th hole,

absent a walker or an acrobat,
three taut wires carving apart

gray clouds, a sudsy sink
upside down

with birds flying
into it.

GUILLOTINE EBULLIENCE

The collective horrors
Out of the way, waiting.

It's a full assault today;
Fine little threads.

But already,
I see:

There's too much cutting here.
Too many necks shaved.

I'll have to strip it all down, again,
Like the rest.

I'm my own executioner;
my problem is that I keep the heads

In constant view, dripping perfect lakes —
They say to me:

Look at the lives you've lived.
Look at who remembers them.

LOW TRAIN SIREN.

This fenced window
with blue-gray dirt
on the sill. Yellow light,
the roof of another
house, leaking
down brown planks.

Train horn bellows
right through the fence
and thorny
rasps of birds cracking
at one another. Green leaf
shake rolls shadows
out of stillness, out of
recognition, onto
the tiled floor
and the bathroom sink
stained with a rust aura
around the drain, a miscarried
sunset like a piss stain frozen
to the porcelain; shadows

belt the window,
the rectangular ledge,
the molding and plaster

suggest another place
altogether: Ireland,
a rowhouse in England,
a small valley village.

The sink drips a tiny chime
over the rust aura; the train
stops.

Blake Edward Hamilton holds an MFA in Creative Writing from Naropa University, and currently teaches college English. His work has appeared in *World Literature Today Magazine: Windmill, NPR, The Guerrilla Literary Magazine, The Bombay Gin Literary Journal, Punch Drunk Press,* and *SoboGhoso Press,* among others. He frequently travels, spending his time between the deserts of New Mexico and Paris, France as often as possible.